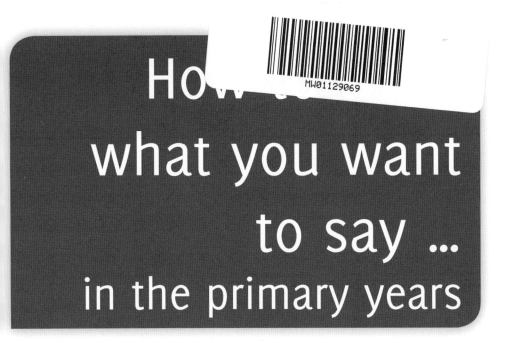

How to say what you want to say ... in the primary years

a guide for primary students who
know what they want to say
but can't find the words

Catherine Black and Patricia Hipwell

Literacy p.d.
practical, relevant professional development

logonliteracy

Linked to the skills of the Australian Curriculum

First published 2014

National Library of Australia Cataloguing-in-Publication entry
Authors: Black, Catherine and Hipwell, Patricia
Title: How to write what you want to say ... in the primary years: a guide for primary
                  students who know what they want to say but can't find the words /
                  Catherine Black and Patricia Hipwell.
ISBN: 9781925046489 (paperback)
Subjects: Authorship.
                  Creative writing (Primary education)
Other Authors/Contributors:
                  Hipwell, Patricia, author.
Dewey Number: 808.02

Typeset in Delicious 10 pt.

Text and cover design: Watson Ferguson & Company
Editing and proofreading: Catherine Comiskey

Note: Text examples of the writing skill have been created to demonstrate that skill. Possible inaccuracies and out-of-date information in these texts are acknowledged by the authors and do not detract from the validity of their inclusion.

Printed and bound by Watson Ferguson & Company, Salisbury, Queensland, Australia

contents

dedication

To our sisters – both bright, wonderful women who would have greatly appreciated this book as children.

introduction

Catherine Black of **Literacy P.D.** and Patricia Hipwell of **logonliteracy** have written this guide for beginning and developing writers in the primary years. It is a starting point for students to find the language they need for the many purposes of writing.

The book is set out in a double-page format:

- The **first page** has a definition of the **writing skill**; **key task words** that link to the skill; and the **sentence starters** for that skill.

- The **second page** has the words or phrases for **connecting ideas**; an **example** of the **skill**; **questions**; and a **graphic organiser** to help with planning for writing.

How to write what you want to say … in the primary years:
a guide for primary students who know what they want to say but can't find the words provides parents, teachers and students with a unique tool for improving writing.

note for teachers
The **writing skills** in this book are the main ones prescribed by the Australian Curriculum. The authors have trawled through the curriculum documents and identified the kinds of writing expected of primary students. This book will support students as they develop these writing skills.

key terms and ideas defined

connectives   words or phrases that link ideas within sentences
                         or from one sentence to the next

formal language   the language of writing not speaking; the language
                         of school subjects; grammar, spelling and
                         punctuation are important

graphic organiser   a diagram that assists with planning for writing

key task words   words in questions that indicate how you should
                         answer the question

modality   expressing how likely, how often, how important
                         or how possible things may be

questions to help   questions that will help students to develop the
                         writing skill

sentence starter   the opening clause or phrase of a sentence

writing skill   the purpose of writing: includes such purposes as
                         describing, retelling, comparing and explaining

analysing

meaning:
looking at the parts of something and showing how the parts connect to each other

key task words linked to *analyse*:
describe, interpret, break down, compare

sentence starters

... could be broken down in the following way/s:

The difference between the ways the two characters see the situation is ...

... would happen if ... were taken away/added.

... are responsible for a number of ...

... is a fact because ..., whereas ... is an opinion because ...

There is a strong connection between ... and ...

... is made up of many parts. These include: ...

If ... were taken away, then ... would happen.

... is connected to ...

... is more important than ...

The most important feature of ... is ...

Many factors lead to the problem of ...

This is because ...

connecting ideas within and between sentences

all	consist/s of	is made up of
also	especially	provided that
as well as	if ..., then ...	so
because	in addition	since
between	is composed of	than

Rabbits in Australia

Rabbits **are responsible for a number of** environmental problems in Australia. Rabbits have caused more damage *than* almost any other pest in Australia. They have had a serious impact on the environment, *especially* on Australian farms. *Since* rabbits were introduced, a number of small native animals have become endangered, including the bilby and yellow-footed rock wallaby. **This is because** rabbits eat their food and compete with them for space and burrows. *In addition*, rabbits attract predators such as foxes and wild dogs, which attack native animals. These predators *also* attack farm animals such as lambs and calves.

Rabbits have *also* had a devastating effect on native plants. These introduced animals graze plants so low to the ground that they have no chance of regenerating (growing back). They ringbark trees or dig up the roots of plants for moisture. They eat seedlings, preventing the plants from growing back. This loss of plants has meant that many places do not have enough plant cover and this leads to soil erosion. Soil erosion and plant damage have a major impact on farms. **When** rabbits **are removed from** an area, the grass grows back and the land recovers.

questions to help you analyse

- What information do I have? Do I need more information?
- What do I have to analyse?
- What are the parts of the topic? How are they connected?
- What would happen if one of the parts were changed? How would everything else be affected?
- What do I have to do when I analyse?

planning for analysing

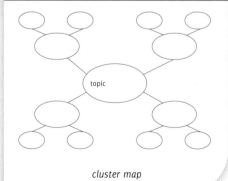

cluster map

arguing or persuading

meaning:

giving an opinion on a topic and trying to persuade others of your point of view by giving evidence and using persuasive techniques

key task words linked to _argue_ or _persuade_:

debate, discuss, justify

sentence starters

My opinion is that ...

I strongly believe that ...

I think/believe that ...

I think there are many reasons to support my point of view, especially ...

I agree/do not agree with ... because ...

... is the evidence, which supports my point of view.

While some people believe ..., I think that ...

My argument is much stronger than ... because ...

There are two sides to this issue and they are ...

Many people believe ...; however, I think that ...

My point of view on this issue is ...

Therefore, there are many reasons ...

connecting ideas within and between sentences

because	however	one reason for
by contrast	in fact	on the other hand
even though	I think	so
furthermore	if …, then	therefore
hence	in addition	whereas

All children should learn to cook

I strongly believe that all children should learn to cook. Cooking allows children to feed themselves and others, which is essential for survival. *If* children can cook, *then* they are less likely to buy unhealthy takeaway or processed food. *Furthermore*, cooking is fun.

Everyone needs to eat, *so* learning to cook is important for children. *If* children know how to cook, *then* they can feed themselves and their family. They do not have to rely on their parents to cook for them. This gives parents a break and, at the same time, improves children's cooking skills. **While some people believe** that cooking is too dangerous for children, I think the earlier they learn to cook, the better.

Learning to cook also leads to healthier food choices. *If* children can cook, *then* they are less likely to buy take-away food. The high fat and sugar content of most take-away food can lead to health problems. Children are more likely to eat food they have made themselves or helped prepare.

In addition, cooking is fun for children. Children enjoy shopping for the ingredients, preparing the food and tasting the results! This is the best part. They love the mixing and chopping, grating and rolling. They enjoy making something other people will eat.

Therefore, there are many reasons children should learn to cook. Cooking means children can survive without relying on their parents. *If* children can cook, they are much less likely to eat takeaway food. *Finally*, cooking is fun.

questions to help you argue or persuade

- What is one point of view?
- What is another point of view?
- What are the reasons for the points of view?
- Which point of view do I agree with and why?
- Do I need more or better information?
- What do I need to do to argue or persuade?

planning for arguing or persuading

topic		
reason for	reason for	reason for

contrast connectives: on the other hand, whereas, however, by contrast, even though, etc.

reason against	reason against	reason against

reasons for and against

5

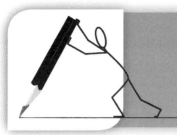

classifying

meaning:

to sort items into categories or groups because they have things in common

key task words linked to *classify*:

sort, arrange

sentence starters

There are (number) main groups of ...

In this group of ... are ...

Another group of ... is ...

The items in this group have ... in common.

There are (number) categories of ...

In this group, ... is the odd one out because ...

We classify ... according to ...

Because ... and ... are similar, they are in the same group.

I would put ... in the same group as ... because ...

A, B and C have ... in common; therefore, they go together.

... belongs to this category of ...

... are in the next group.

In the smallest/largest group are the ...

connecting ideas within and between sentences

according to	in general	such as
and these are	in most cases	tend to be
commonly	mainly	there are examples
for the most part	normally	typically
in common	so	without exception

The five food groups

There are five main groups of food and, to eat well, we need to eat a balanced diet that includes food from all five food groups. **The five main food groups** are: breads, cereals and grains; fruits and vegetables; meat, chicken, fish, eggs and meat alternatives; dairy foods; and fats, sugars and salt. These five food groups are often presented as a triangular chart or portions on a plate.

The images show what types of foods we need the most and least, compared with the other food groups. *In most cases*, we need grains more than other foods. Fruits and vegetables **are in the next group**, while dairy and meat, eggs, fish, chicken and meat alternatives are in the third and fourth groups. **In the smallest group are the** fats, sugars and salt. Foods *such as* chocolate and hot chips should be rare treats; *for the most part*, we should not eat much of them.

NB. Images not included

questions to help you classify

- What things are alike and could be grouped?
- Does everything fit into the groups I have?
- What do the things in each group have in common?
- Can I group my items in any other way?
- What have I learned about classifying?

planning for classifying

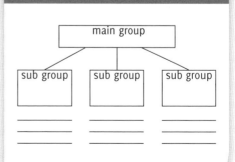

classification table

comparing

meaning:
looking at two or more things and saying how they are similar and different

key task words linked to *compare*:
contrast, distinguish

sentence starters

... is similar to ... because

... is different from ... because ...

Both ... and ... have/are ...

There are similarities between ... and ...

The main difference between ... and ... is ...

... and ... are similar because they both ...

This is similar to ...

This is different from ...

... and ... are alike/different because...

Therefore, ... are similar in that ...

   Therefore, ... are similar because ...

   This is/was the main difference between them.

connecting ideas within and between sentences

alike/like/just like	compared with	more/most
also	different	nevertheless
although	even though	similarly
as well as	however	though
but	in the same way	whereas

Solids and liquids

In the experiment, we started with butter, chocolate and candle wax at 22 degrees Celsius. Chocolate, butter and candle wax **are similar in that** they are solid at this temperature. We had to use an element to heat up each of them to note the temperature at which they changed from solid to liquid. The butter turned to liquid at 50 degrees, *whereas* the chocolate melted at 35 degrees. *However*, the candle wax needed the *most* heat, turning to liquid at 65 degrees. Therefore, all materials **are similar because** they turned to liquid when heated. They needed *different* amounts of heat *though,* to turn to liquid. **This is the main difference between them.**

questions to help you compare

- Which things am I comparing?
- What is it about them that I am comparing?
- What is similar?
- What is different?
- When would I compare two things?
- Why would I compare two things?
- What have I learned about comparison?

planning for comparing two things

I am comparing .... with ....

how different?	how the same?	how different?

3 column Venn

contrasting

meaning:
looking at two or more things and saying how they are different

key task words linked to *contrast*:
compare, distinguish

sentence starters

Even though they are both ..., they are/were different.

... is different from ... because ...

The main difference between ... and ... is/was ...

This is different from ...

... and ... are different because ...

... and ... are not alike.

... and ... have nothing in common.

While ... is like ..., ... is like ...

These two things are dissimilar.

These two things are very different.

... and ... look similar; however, they are different.

connecting ideas within and between sentences

alternatively	however	other differences include
although	in spite of this	unlike
by contrast	on the one hand	whereas
even so	on the other hand	while
even though	or	yet

Tyrannosaurus and triceratops

The tyrannosaurus and the triceratops are two well-known dinosaurs. **Even though they were both** from the late Cretaceous period, **they were different**. The tyrannosaurus was longer and heavier than the triceratops. The tyrannosaurus was 12 metres long, *whereas* the triceratops was only 9 metres. The tyrannosaurus weighed 7 tonnes, *while* the triceratops weighed 5 tonnes. **They also looked different.** The triceratops had three horns on its face and a spiny frill on the back of its head. It walked on all four legs. *On the other hand*, the tyrannosaurus stood on its hind legs. It had small, stubby arms and a large head with sharp teeth.

The main difference between the tyrannosaurus **and** the triceratops **was** their diet. The triceratops was a vegetarian (plant-eater), *unlike* the carnivorous (meat-eating) tyrannosaurus. This meant that the tyrannosaurus was much more dangerous than the triceratops, *even though* the triceratops looked fierce with its three horns.

questions to help you contrast

- Which things am I contrasting?
- What is it about them that I am contrasting?
- What is different?
- Why or how are they different?
- Are they alike in any way?
- What have I learned about contrasting?

planning for contrasting

	object 1	object 2
characteristic 1		
characteristic 2		
characteristic 3		

contrast matrix

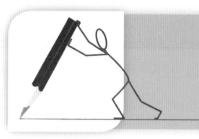

describing

sentence starters

The features of ... are ...

... looks/sounds/feels/tastes/smells like ...

... has several features, which include ...

... has characteristics that make it interesting/important.

... is made of ...

At the centre/edge of the ...

The character in the story has a ... personality.

One of the characteristics of ... is ...

If we look closely at ..., we can see ...

... is one of ...

... has ... as well as ...

connecting ideas within and between sentences

all	besides	several
along with	firstly, secondly, finally	such as
also	for example	this/these feature/s
and	many	too
as well as being a/an	represent/s/ing	what's more

The Torres Strait Islander Flag

The Torres Strait Islander Flag **is one of** Australia's official flags. The green panels at the top and bottom of the flag represent the land, *and* the blue panel in the middle *represents* the sea. The black lines dividing the panels *represent* the Torres Strait Islander people.

At the centre of the flag is a dancer's headdress called a dhari, which is a symbol of all Torres Strait Islanders.

If we look closely, we can see a white five-pointed star underneath the dhari. *As well as being an* important symbol for navigating the sea, the star *also represents* the island groups in the Torres Strait. The star and the dhari are white, *representing* peace.

questions to help you describe

- What am I describing?
- Which parts will I write/speak about?
- What do I see, feel, hear, taste or touch?
- In my own words, what is …?
- Which adjectives and adverbs will I use to describe …?
- When would I describe something?

planning for describing

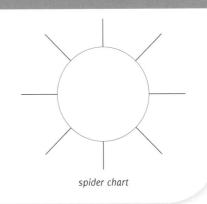

spider chart

evaluating

meaning:
weighing up the value or worth of something

key task words linked to *evaluate*:
assess, criticise, examine

sentence starters

The best feature of ... is/was that it ...

We should keep this because ...

It worked well when ...; however, ...

If we changed ..., then ...

To improve ..., I would need to ...

Although we did ..., we need to ...

... is better than ... because ...

... is not as good as ... because ...

On balance, ... is better.

Another way of doing ... is to ...

Another good thing about ... is/was that it was ...

I could also look at ...

While ... looked better, I was pleased with mine because ...

connecting ideas within and between sentences

although	however	the reason being
as a result	if … then …	therefore
because	in spite of this	when …, then …
better/worse	rather than	whereas
greater/fewer	so	while

My paper aeroplane

Our project was to research and design our own paper aeroplane. We tested our planes to see how far each one flew. I chose a dart-style plane *because* I had read that a thinner plane would create less drag than a traditional paper plane. **The best feature** of my plane **was that it** flew for a long distance, *whereas* some of the other planes flew for a much shorter distance. **Another good thing about** my plane **was that it was** easy to make. There were instructions on the Internet about how to make a dart plane. **While** some of the planes made by other children in the class **looked better, I was pleased with mine because** it flew so well.

To improve my dart plane, **I would need to** use thicker, stronger paper. I found that the wings would sometimes fold down instead of sticking out as they were supposed to do. **I could also look at** other plane designs and compare various options *rather than* staying with my first choice.

questions to help you evaluate

- How will I evaluate my work?
- Can I do this better?
- What do I need to improve?
- What can I make that is new and/or improved?
- Should I try it another way?
- Why is evaluation important?

planning for evaluating

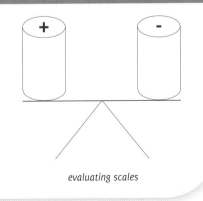

evaluating scales

explaining-how

meaning:
making the reader understand the process of how something works or occurs, usually in a series of steps

key task words linked to *explain*:
account for, interpret

sentence starters

The first thing that happens is ...

... do this by ...

... is like this because ...

... works by ...

... do this so that it/they can ...

Firstly, you must ...

The next thing that happens is ...

This leads to ...

When ..., then ...

... causes this to ...

connecting ideas within and between sentences

and so	if ..., then	therefore
and this leads to	is because	this is how
as a result of	so	when ..., then
consequently	the effect of	which is caused by
due to	the reason for	which leads to

How do bees make honey?

Honey is an energy food *because* it contains sugar that the body can use quickly. Bees make honey. **The first thing that happens is** worker bees from the hive gather nectar—a sweet, sticky liquid—from flowers. They **do this by** sucking the nectar with long tube-like tongues. The nectar goes into the bee's honey stomach, where enzymes (chemicals that cause changes) change the nectar into two types of sugar—fructose and glucose.

When the bees return to the hive, they **then** spit out the honey into hexagon-shaped compartments called cells. They seal these cells with wax caps. *Because* it is warm in the hive, the water from the honey evaporates, *and so* the honey becomes thicker and stronger in flavour.

questions to help you explain how

- What event or idea do I need to explain?
- What do I already know that will help me to explain my topic?
- Where will I find information to help with my explanation?
- How can I explain what I hear/taste/see/feel/smell?
- Why would I explain how something happens?

planning for explaining how

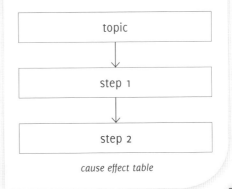

cause effect table

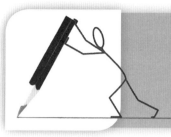

explaining–why

meaning:
making the reader understand why something is the way it is by giving reasons

key task words linked to _explain_:
account for, interpret

sentence starters

The reason we have ... is that ...

There are many reasons for ...

... is/are caused by ...

An effect of ... is ...

The major cause of ... is ...

... happened because of ...

Because ..., several things have occurred.

The main reason that ... occurs is ...

... causes ..., which leads to ...

... are most likely to occur if/when ...

This is why ...

This is because ...

connecting ideas within and between sentences

and so	even though	the reason for
and this leads to	if …, then	therefore
as a result of	is because	when …, then
consequently	is that	which is caused by
due to	so	which leads to

Why do we have day and night?

The reason we have day and night **is that** the Earth rotates. *When* the earth rotates, *then* it spins on its axis—an imaginary line passing between the North and South Poles.

The Earth spins slowly all the time; however, we do not feel it moving *because* it turns smoothly and at the same speed. It takes a whole day — 24 hours — for the Earth to make a complete turn.

At any given time only half of the Earth faces the Sun. This part, *therefore*, has day. The Sun is the source of light during the day. The other half of the Earth faces away from the Sun, *so* it receives no light. This half has night.

Even though it looks as though the sun moves across the sky during the day, the Sun does not move. It is the Earth turning that makes it seem as though the Sun is moving. **This is why** we call the start of the day "sunrise" and the end of the day "sunset".

questions to help you explain why

- What event or idea do I need to explain?
- What do I already know that will help me to explain my topic?
- Where will I find information to help with my explanation?
- How can I explain what I hear/taste/see/feel/smell?
- Why would I explain why something happens?

planning for explaining why

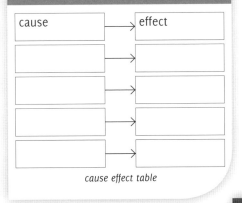

cause effect table

generalising

meaning:
developing a broad statement that can apply to many things

key task words linked to *generalise*:
summarise, outline

sentence starters

Generally speaking, ... is true.

For the most part, ... applies.

Overall, ... is the case.

As a rule, ... can be said.

Mostly, ... is what is said/done/heard.

Broadly speaking, we can say that ...

In most cases, ... applies.

... is more likely than ...

... has the same general idea as ...

A general statement that applies to ... is ...

It is/was common for ...

connecting ideas within and between sentences

broadly speaking	in general	most often
by and large	in most cases	often
commonly	mainly	on the whole
generally	many	regularly
in common	most/ly	usually

European settlement and its effects on Indigenous Australians

Europeans began to live in Australian from 1788. Indigenous Australians had lived here for 50,000 years or longer. Indigenous people were not well treated by the new arrivals. **It was common** for the settlers to move Indigenous people off their land into places where the Europeans did not want to live. *Usually,* these were the very hot and dry parts of Australia. When Indigenous people fought against the control of the Europeans, *many* of them were arrested and, *in most cases*, they were imprisoned. They were expected to take on European ways and forget about their traditional ways of living.

For the most part, Indigenous people were worse off than before European settlement. *Many* people today believe that Indigenous people are still poorly treated when compared with non-Indigenous people. All around the world, *many* Indigenous people have suffered because of settlement by other nations.

NB. Graphs not included inside the box

questions to help you generalise

- What is important here?
- How can I say the same thing in a more general way?
- What else has the same general pattern?
- Which details will I leave out?
- Why is it sometimes better to generalise than give details?

planning for generalising

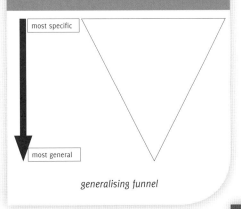

generalising funnel

giving more detail

meaning:
looking at something in a more detailed way by giving more information

key task words linked to *giving more detail*:
examine, illustrate, justify

sentence starters

A detailed look at ... shows ...

The information is correct and supported by the following evidence: ...

This finding is valid because ...

One interpretation of the findings could be ...

If the topic is placed under the microscope, then it becomes clear that ...

Looking closely, it is easy to see that ...

... is additional information about ...

Examples of ... include ...

... is evidence that supports the point of view.

Additional information, such as ..., backs up ...

It is clear that ...

A/Another feature of ... is that ...

connecting ideas within and between sentences

also	for example/instance	obviously
clearly	in detail	reveals
closely	indicates	shows
even if	is more than	such as
firstly	means	this means that

Friendship

Friendship *is more than* just liking each other and having fun together. **A detailed look at friendship** shows that there are many things required to make it work properly.

Firstly, friends have to have something in common. It can be something they are both interested in, *such as* dinosaurs or *Star Wars*, or something they both enjoy doing, *such as* dancing, skipping or playing soccer. Having something in common makes it easier to enjoy spending time together.

It is clear that friendship also needs trust. You have to be able to trust your friends. *For instance*, you need to be able to tell your friends secrets and trust that they will not tell anyone else. You *also* need to trust that your friends will do what they say they will do, so you can rely on them. **Another feature of friendship is that** friends are loyal to one another. *This means that* they will stick by you no matter what. *For example*, if someone is saying hurtful things about you, your friend will stick up for you. They stay your friend *even if* you do something embarrassing or you are not popular.

Friendship *also* needs good talking and listening skills. True friends take turns talking and listening. They wait to hear the other person's opinions and ideas. They tell you what they are thinking and doing, and ask you questions.

questions to help you give more detail

- About what do I have to give more detail?
- What ideas might I add to my writing or speaking?
- What more can I say/write?
- Where might I look for more detail?
- Why is it important to give more detail?

planning for giving more detail

iceberg for giving more detail

Within the image: main idea / more detail about the main idea (explanation, examples, evidence, etc)

inferring

meaning:
to work something out even though it is not said or written

key task words linked to *infer*:
interpret, account for

sentence starters

It/this means that ...

It/this could mean that ...

Reading between the lines suggests ...

The answer to the question is not obvious; however, I think that ...

In the story, the ... says, '...' and this means, '...'

The evidence in the text to support ... is where it says, '...'

This is how we know ...

This is why we know ...

It is likely that ... because ...

I think the author wants the reader to ...

I think the moral or message of ... is ...

Another message from the story is ...

connecting ideas within and between sentences

because	it appears	since
clearly	it is clear/unclear	therefore
due to	it seems	this is how
even/though/even though	means	this is why
hence	reveals	though

The Lion and the Mouse

I think the main moral or message of 'The Lion and the Mouse' is that *even* small friends can be helpful. When the mouse tells the lion that she might be useful to him some time in the future, he laughs. *Even though* the idea that a tiny mouse can help a lion seems unlikely, I think the author wants the reader to know that it is possible. In the story, the lion says, "What? A tiny mouse helping the king of the beasts?" This means that he does not believe her. At the end of the story, *though*, the little mouse saves the lion by gnawing through the ropes that trap him. *Even though* the mouse was small, she was able to help save the lion's life.

Another message from the story is that one good turn deserves another. *Because* the lion is kind to the mouse and lets her go, the mouse helps him.

NB. fable not included

questions to help you infer

- What information do I have?
- What do I have to find out?
- Do I know where to look for the answer?
- Is the answer here, in the head or hidden?
- What do I have to do when I infer?

planning for inferring

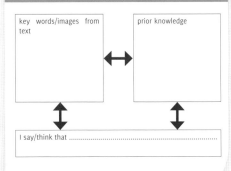

inference organiser

interpreting

meaning:
to explain the meaning or significance of something

key task words linked to *interpret*:
infer, explain

sentence starters

It means that ...

The figures clearly show that ...

The text says, '...' and this means, '...'

The evidence in the text to support ..., is where it says, '...'

The picture shows ..., and this means ...

It appears that ...

This increase/decrease seems to be due to ...

There is a pattern in the information and it is ...

... could mean ..., or it could mean ...

There is more than one interpretation of ...

The data shows ... and this means ...

One interpretation could be ...

Another interpretation could be ...

because	hence	the reason for
clearly show/s	it appears	therefore
due to	it can be	this is how/why
even though	it seems	this means
from this/these	rather than	which adds to

Childhood obesity

Childhood obesity is a health problem in Australia. While only 5% of children were overweight or obese in the 1960s, by 1985 this had risen to 10%. Between 1985 and 1995, the rate of overweight children doubled, and obesity tripled. Twenty-three per cent of children now suffer from obesity or being overweight. This is almost one in four Australian children. **These figures clearly show** that childhood obesity is rising. It is a major health problem in Australia today.

This increase seems to be due to children's lack of exercise and the sort of food they are eating. Children are spending more time playing computer games and watching TV *rather than* playing in the back yard or participating in sports. Forty-five per cent of children watch more than 10 hours of TV per week. **It appears that** people also now eat out or buy take-away food much more than they did twenty years ago. Fast food is more readily available. Unfortunately, the fat and sugar content of these foods is high, *which adds to* childhood obesity.

NB: graphs are not included

questions to help you interpret

- What information do I have?
- What does the information mean?
- Do I observe a pattern?
- Do I need more information to interpret what I have been given?
- What do I have to do when I interpret?

planning for interpreting

what I'm told
what it means
what I'm told
what it means

interpreting table

justifying

meaning:
giving reasons for a decision or conclusion that has been made; answering the question, 'Why?'

key tasks words linked to *justify*:
account for, explain, support

sentence starters

There are many reasons ...

Consequently, it would seem better to ...

There is, therefore, no doubt/some doubt/much doubt about ...

... is a better option because ...

The best decision is ...

Fact, rather than opinion, supports the decision to ...

... is a good idea because ...

For now, ... is the better choice because ...

... took this course of action because ...

The character did/said ... because ...

The best course of action is ...

connecting ideas within and between sentences

although	even though	reinforces
as a result of	firstly, secondly, finally	so
as though	for example/instance	supports
because of	in this situation	therefore
better/worse	is preferred because	under the circumstances

Feeding animals in national parks

There are many reasons people should not feed animals in national parks. *Even though* feeding wildlife might seem as though it is helping the animals, it is actually causing harm. *Firstly*, the food people feed native animals is often not good for them. It does not contain the correct vitamins and minerals. *Therefore*, this can make some animals ill.

Feeding the animals in national parks can make wildlife dependent on humans, rather than finding food for themselves. This makes them unable to survive on their own. *Because of* regular feeding by humans in national parks, some animals have become a nuisance. Some have even become aggressive and, *therefore*, dangerous. On Fraser Island, *for example*, dingoes regularly fed by humans have been known to attack campers. **There is no doubt** that humans in national parks should not feed the animals. **The best course of action is** to keep human food away from wildlife.

questions to help you justify

- Which is the best decision and why?
- What are the pluses and minuses of my choice?
- Is my justification fact or opinion?
- If it is an opinion, where is my support?
- Why should I justify my choice or decision?

planning for justifying

decision:

justification:

because

because

because

justification flow chart

listing

meaning:
arranging items in order, usually one after the other

key task words linked to *listing*:
recount, retell, arrange

sentence starters

I will need the following items:

The first/second/third thing to bring/use/remember is ...

These are the main points to remember:

Some examples/non-examples are:

Do not forget to include the following:

I must include these items:

I will not need ... because ...

... might/must have these features/characteristics:

To make ..., I will need to collect:

The mains events in the story are:

The materials for the model/project are ...

connecting ideas within and between sentences

1,2,3,4,5	finally	next
after that	first/ly	not only … but also
along with	followed by	second/ly
also	in addition to	some
and	lastly	third/ly

Living things

Living things **must have these characteristics:**

- able to move
- able to reproduce (make more organisms like themselves)
- able to grow
- need food

Living things **might have these characteristics:**

- be used as food by other organisms
- able to fly
- able to walk or run
- have leaves, roots and stems

Some examples of living things are:

- people
- fish
- trees
- weeds
- insects
- snails

Some non examples (non-living things) are:

- rocks
- metals
- sound
- air
- dirt
- cars
- TVs

questions to help you list

- What do I need to put on my list?
- What can I leave off my list?
- Can I arrange my items in any order?
- When would I make a list?

planning for listing

	list
1.	_____
2.	_____
3.	_____
4.	_____
5.	_____
6.	_____
7.	_____
8.	_____
9.	_____
10.	_____

locating and retrieving information

meaning:
finding the information that is stated; the information is 'right there'

key task words linked to *locating* and *retrieving* information:
find, locate, summarise

sentence starters

In the text, it states that …

The story is set in …

The main character in the story lives in …

The main event occurs during …

It says that …; therefore, we know that …

When … happens, then … follows.

… caused … to happen

… are the key words in the text.

This text is about …

The main events in (name of person's) life were …

… happened before/after …

connecting ideas within and between sentences

and	that	those
here	then	what
it	there	when
says that	these	which
states that	this	who

Pemulwuy

Who was Pemulwuy? Pemulwuy was a great Australian aboriginal warrior who fought against the British invaders from 1780 to 1802.

Why did Pemulwuy fight the British? Pemulwuy was trying to protect his land and the Eora people.

How did Pemulwuy fight the British? Pemulwuy did not have a big army. Instead, he organised small groups to raid the settlements and camps. *This* type of fighting is called guerrilla warfare.

Describe some of Pemulwuy's fights. Pemulwuy's first known attack was against John McIntyre. John McIntyre, the governor's gamekeeper, was believed to have killed a number of aboriginal people, so Pemulwuy speared him. He later died, and Pemulwuy was declared an outlaw. The British staged revenge attacks against the Eora people, and Pemulwuy fought back with more attacks on farms and settlements. He began to use fire as a weapon.

What happened to Pemulwuy in 1797? Pemulwuy was shot and captured during an attack on Parramatta. Despite his injuries, he managed to escape. The Eora people were amazed, believing Pemulwuy must have turned into a crow to fly through the prison bars.

What was the governor's opinion of Pemulwuy? *When* Pemulwuy was shot dead in 1802, Governor King wrote, "Although a terrible pest to the colony, he was a brave and independent character."

questions to help you to locate and retrieve information

- What are the key words in the question?
- Am I looking for words that mean the same as the words in the question?
- Where will I look for the answer?
- Do I need to look in more than one place?
- Where will I be able to use the skill of locating and retrieving information?

planning for locating and retrieving information

the 5Ws question mark

making connections

meaning:
making meaning by connecting ideas with own experiences and across paragraphs and illustrations in text

key task words linked to *making connections*:
link, connect, draw together

sentence starters

The purpose of the text/illustration is to …

In the first part, the author says …, and then he/she says …

The author has included …, so that …

This was similar to the …

A similar thing happened to me when …

The text tells the reader …, whereas the illustration shows the reader …

The author has used the word/phrase to show the reader that …

Our teacher told us that …

I know a person like this character and s/he …

This reminds me of another book I read. It was about …

The difference between … and …, though, was that …

In real life … happens too.

… brought in some … that …

connecting ideas within and between sentences

and	that	those
here	then	what
it	there	when
says that	they	where
so that	these/this	while

Silkworms

As part of our science unit on life cycles, we have been looking after silkworms, *and* watching how they change and grow. *When* we first got them, the silkworms were just tiny eggs. *Then* they hatched into little caterpillars. They ate through mulberry leaves *and* became big and fat. **This was similar to the** video we watched about the life cycle of a butterfly, where the caterpillars hatched out of tiny eggs and grew. **The difference between caterpillars and our silkworms, though, was that** our silkworms spun a special silk cocoon instead of a chrysalis.

Our teacher told us that silkworms are used in factories to make silk. *So that* the silk strand does not break, workers kill the pupa while it is still in its cocoon. Lucy **brought in some** silk scarves **that** her mum had brought back from overseas. They were very soft, and much smoother than our silkworms' cocoons.

When our silkworms came out of their cocoons, *they* were white moths. *While* the butterflies in the video we watched could fly around, our silkworm moths could not fly. Eventually they died after laying some more eggs. **This** whole cycle took a long time — almost the whole term!

questions to help you make connections

- What do I already know about this?
- Has something similar happened to me?
- How many parts are there in the text?
- What is the purpose of each part of the text?
- Why is it important to make connections?

planning for making connections

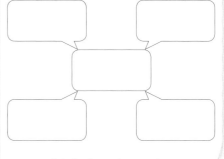

bringing it together template

35

making a decision

meaning:
examining a number of options and coming to a conclusion about the best one

key task words linked to *making a decision*:
decide, state, conclude

sentence starters

The evidence supports the decision to ...

... is the best decision because ...

All the evidence means that ... is the best decision.

To make this decision, I looked at ...

There is, therefore, no doubt that ... is the best ...

Consequently, it would seem better to do ... than ...

I/We had/have to choose from ...

The decision is not an easy one to make; however, ...

Overall, ... is the best decision.

Finally, I had to choose ...

I then had to work out ...

Not only ..., but it also ...

connecting ideas within and between sentences

all things considered	I decided	on condition that
also	if … then …	therefore
because	in the end	these include
finally	in addition	was to decide
however	is recommended	without a doubt

Choosing the best material for a baby's toy

My job *was to decide* which material would be the best to use for a baby's toy. **I had to choose** from wood, plastic, fabric or metal. **To make this decision, I looked at** the properties of each material. **I then had to work out** which of these properties would be the safest and most suitable for a baby.

I decided against metal straight away. **Not only** is it too hard and heavy for a baby's toy, **but it also** conducts heat and electricity. Fabric seemed a safer material because it is soft and insulating. *However*, I thought a baby's toy should be waterproof because babies dribble so much.

Finally, I had to choose between wood and plastic. Both are strong and long-lasting, and neither conduct heat or electricity. *In the end*, I chose plastic. Plastic is more waterproof than wood. *In addition*, plastic can be dyed different colours or made transparent (see through). It is also lighter than wood. **There is, therefore, no doubt** that plastic **is the best** material to use for a baby's toy.

questions to help you make a decision

- What I am trying to decide?
- What are my choices?
- What are the criteria for making this decision?
- How do I know that my decision is the best one?
- What do I have to do when I make a decision?

planning for making a decision

alternative 1		alternative 2	
plus	minus	plus	minus
final decision			

decision making matrix

providing support

meaning:
giving evidence or examples to support an idea, fact or opinion

key task words linked to *providing support*:
Illustrate, prove, refer

sentence starters

There is much evidence to support ...

A detailed examination of ... shows that ...

... supports the point that I have made.

The evidence to support ... includes ...

The example of ... makes the argument true.

There are many examples of ... to show ...

The first reason for ... is ...

Another reason is that ...

This/that means there is more/less ...

All of these reasons indicate that ...

connecting ideas within and between sentences

also	for instance	it is clear that
clearly	furthermore	means
closely	indeed	shows
firstly	in detail	such as
for example	indicates	thorough

Composting in schools

There is much evidence to support the benefits of composting in schools. *Firstly*, compost is an excellent way to make use of food scraps, paper, grass clippings and other plant waste created in the school grounds. **This means there is less** garbage to be collected every day, which saves the school money, as well as reducing its carbon footprint. Instead of being added to landfill, this organic matter can be made into compost. The compost is then used as fertiliser on the school gardens.

Using compost on the gardens *also* improves the soil. *For example*, compost rich soil attracts worms that help plants grow. School children can help collect and make the compost and dig it in. *Furthermore*, composting is a fun, practical way to learn to, "reduce, re-use and recycle". **All of these reasons indicate** that schools should make composting part of the school day.

questions to help you provide support

- Do I know what is meant by evidence and examples?
- How do I support my facts?
- What ideas will I add to my writing or speaking?
- What more can I say/write about?
- Where might I look for support for my point of view?
- Why is it sometimes necessary to provide support?

planning for providing support

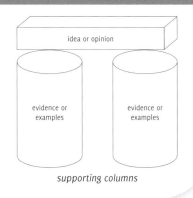

supporting columns

putting it together

meaning:
connecting ideas across text or drawing ideas from several sources

key task words linked to *putting it together*:
draw together, conclude, summarise

sentence starters

... combines pictures and words to get the key message across.

Writer A states ..., whereas writer B states ...

The purpose of the visual text is to show ..., and the message is the same as/different from the writing.

This information about ... is more important than the information about ...

From Source A, I learnt ..., and this is different from the information in Source B.

The bold text ... reads ...

The best solution to the problem is ... because it takes into account several sources of information.

Everything points to ...

All the information suggests that ...

All the features combine to make ...

This shows the reader an example of ...

alternatively	even though	on the other hand
backs up	however	reinforces this/is reinforced by
combines	in summary	to blend the ideas
coming together	joins/joined	together
differ/s from	merged	while

The bullying poster

The bullying poster **combines pictures and words to get the key message across. The purpose of this poster** is to encourage people to stand up to bullies rather than joining in or doing nothing. It is aimed at anyone who is nearby *while* someone is being bullied. **The bold text at the top of the poster reads,** "Bystanders!" and the word, 'you' is repeated. It reads, "If you see someone being bullied, you can help." At the bottom of the poster, this message is *reinforced by* a picture of a hand pointing at the reader, and the words, "If you join in or do nothing, YOU are a bully too!" The poster also shows a picture of a big boy going through a younger boy's bag to steal his lunch, *while* two other boys look on. **This shows the reader an example of** bystanders doing nothing, which *backs up* the main message. **All the information suggests that** everyone should help to stop bullying.

NB bullying poster not included

questions to help you put it together

- Where in the text do I need to look for my answer?
- What does each source tell me?
- Are the sources giving me different information?
- Which information is important/relevant?
- What do I have to do when I put information together?

planning for putting it together

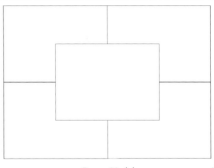

Frayer Model

reflecting

meaning:
looking back and thinking about what something means to
you or the effect that it has on you as a learner

key task words linked to *reflection*:
consider, think about, reflect on

sentence starters

When I thought about ..., I realised ...

... was similar to/different from ...

This was important/unimportant because ...

Thinking carefully about ... made me want to ...

I know why ... worked. It was because ...

From this, I have learned ...

I can now explain ..., because I have thought about it.

... was important/meaningful/useful because ...

I noticed ... and this meant ...

When I asked a question, it was because ...

Our group realised/did not realise that ...

I like/do not like working in a group because ...

connecting ideas within and between sentences

alternatively	due to	might be
arose from	explained by	previously
at first	happened when	related to
because	is probably	this shows
could be	later	when ... then

Our performance

Our group had to prepare and perform the poem, 'Time Passes' with actions and costumes.

It was difficult to agree *at first, because* everyone had different ideas. *Later,* we each took on specific roles, and that worked well. **From this, I have learned** that groups will only work if there is one leader and everyone has something to do.

Our group realised that working out what the poem meant was important *because* that guided our performance. We spent time discussing the poem's meaning before we made any decisions about how we could present it. **This was useful because** it made our performance much better.

Working in a group was different from performing or speaking on my own. **I like working in a group because** it is more fun, but it is easier to work on my own.

questions to help you reflect

- On what am I reflecting?
- What happened during the event?
- Why do I think these things happened?
- How might someone else interpret what happened?
- What does the event mean to me?
- Why is reflection an important thing to do?

planning for reflecting

	plus	minus	interesting
event/feature			
event/feature			
event/feature			

PMI chart

retelling or recounting

meaning:
arranging events in the order in which they happened;
sequence is important

key task words linked to *retell or recount*:
recall, list, review

The first event that took place was ...

This is/was followed by ...

Much later on in the story, ... happened.

Several days/months/years later, ... took place.

After a long period ... came about.

Up until now, ...

A great deal occurred before/after ...

... led to ...

Meanwhile ... was taking place.

Over the next (time period), ... happened.

From then on ...

connecting ideas within and between sentences

before	during	after
before	and then (use sparingly)	a final point
every time	as	after
first, second, third, etc	at the same time	finally
in the beginning	the next day/week/year/etc	in summary
now that	while	lastly

Simpson and his donkey

Jack Simpson was a famous, brave soldier. His job was to carry soldiers, who had been hurt, back to safety. He landed at Gallipoli with the other ANZACs on 25th April, 1915.

The next day, Simpson saw a donkey and had a good idea. It took two men to carry someone on a stretcher, but if he used a donkey, he could do it on his own. **Up until now,** stretcher teams could usually make up to six trips a day, but with his donkey, Simpson could make twice as many.

From then on, Simpson and his donkey, Duffy, walked through the flying bullets to rescue injured soldiers and carry them back to the medical tent. Simpson did not seem to mind the danger. He whistled and sang *as* he walked. Simpson placed the injured soldier on the donkey's back, *and then* held on to the soldier so he did not fall off.

Over the next 24 days, Simpson rescued 300 injured soldiers. *Finally,* on 19th May, 1915, he was hit in the back by a machine gun bullet and died.

Simpson and his donkey showed the true ANZAC spirit of bravery and mateship. They have become a symbol of ANZAC Day.

questions to help you retell/recount

- What events do I need to put in order?
- Is there more than one way to put the events in order? If so, which will I choose and why?
- What happens when I put the events out of order?
- When do I retell or recount events?

planning for retelling/recounting

Direction: Draw pictures to represent 8 main events. Make sure they are in the order in which they happened (chronological order).

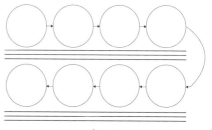

8 events

sequencing

meaning:
giving a series of steps in the order in which they occur

key task words linked to *sequence*:
arrange, list, summarise

sentence starters

The first thing a … must do is …

The next thing to do is …

This is followed by …

After doing this, … must be done.

Before doing …, make sure that you …

Firstly, make sure that you have …

The next step is to …

It does/does not matter if you do … before …

If you do not do things in the correct order, then …

Once you have …, then it is fine to …

If … is done before …, then …

The final step in the sequence is to …

Finally, make sure that you have …

   … can happen at any time.

after	finally	now that
and then (use sparingly)	following	second/secondly
at the same time	lastly	now that
before	meanwhile	then
first/firstly	next	while

Pole-vaulting

Pole-vaulting is a track and field event where athletes use a long, flexible pole to launch themselves over a high bar.

Before the pole vaulter grips the pole, she rubs chalk dust onto her hands. This is so that her hands do not slip, especially if they are sweaty. *Now that* her hands are dry, she can grip the pole. *Then* the pole-vaulter carries and runs with the pole. *Next*, she plants the pole in the ground so that she can take off. **This is followed by a** move called the "pull, turn and push", which takes the vaulter over the bar. *After* the clearance, she lands on the mat.

If she does not clear the bar, then the vaulter is allowed two more attempts *before* she is out of the competition.

questions to help you sequence

- What steps do I need to put in order?
- Is there more than one way to put the steps in order? If so, which will I choose and why?
- What happens when I put the steps out of order?
- When do I sequence steps/events?

planning for sequencing

direction: chart the steps/events that lead to others

flow chart

solving problems

sentence starters

The problem we are trying to solve is ...

The problem with this idea is, however, ...

... is a problem because ...

There are many causes of the problem, and these include: ...

This problem is difficult to solve because ...

One solution to the problem is ...

The first solution tried was ...

To overcome this problem, we must ...

Our challenge, therefore, is/was to come up with other ways to tackle the problem.

While ..., it created other problems.

We thought that ... would be a solution.

Another plan was to ...

We also came up with the idea of ...

Eventually, we decided that the best thing to do was to ...

connecting ideas within and between sentences

a solution is ...	required	therefore
because	results from	that way
but	so	this way
grew out of	solved by	urgent
necessary	tackle the problem	we also decided

The problem with mud outside the classroom

The problem we are trying to solve is the mud outside our classroom. The mud **is a problem because** we keep getting mud from our shoes all over the new carpet. **The main causes of this problem** are rainy days and people walking over the same piece of ground making the ground muddy.

The first solution our class **tried** was to ask everyone to take off their shoes before they came into the classroom. **While** this meant that there was less mud coming inside, **it created other problems.** People came inside either before they took their shoes off, which left mud on the carpet, or they took their shoes off outside, and got their socks wet. There was also a pile of shoes in the doorway, which people tripped over. It also took all of us too long to put our shoes back on whenever we needed to go outside.

Our challenge, therefore, was to come up with other ways to tackle the problem. We thought that cementing or paving the muddy area **would be a solution,** *because* people already use it as a walkway, and it would take away the mud. **The problems with this idea, however,** are that it would be expensive and it would take a long time to complete.

Eventually, we decided that the best thing to do was to put up a temporary fence around the muddy area to stop people walking on it. *That way,* no mud would get onto our shoes. *We also decided* to use a bigger mat just inside the door in case people had mud on their shoes from other places.

questions to help you solve problems

- Have I identified the problem and stated it in my own words?
- How will I tackle the problem?
- Which solution will I suggest or try?
- How will I know if I have been successful?
- Why is it important to solve problems?

planning for problem solving

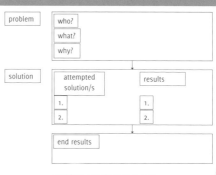

problem solution template 1

summarising

meaning:
briefly stating the main message/idea/subject without details

key task words linked to *summarise*:
outline, review

sentence starters

The main points are …

The key ideas are …

Generally speaking, …

Generally, we have found out … from the information.

The main points are:

… is a main point, whereas … is a detail.

… are the main ideas of the text.

The most important information includes …

… is more significant than …

… is relevant, whereas … is not.

In summary, …

connecting ideas within and between sentences

at a glance	in most cases	secondly
finally	in summary	summing up
firstly	mainly	then
first of all	often	to begin with
in a nutshell	overall	to tie things together

Government in Australia

In summary, Australia has three levels of government—local, state and federal. *Overall,* each level of government holds elections, makes laws for citizens, provides public goods and services, and punishes those who break their laws. **Generally speaking,** each level of government has particular responsibilities. *Firstly,* local government is responsible for providing services within the local area, including maintenance of roads and footpaths; garbage collection; town planning and building regulations; libraries; and maintenance of parks, gardens and swimming pools. *In a nutshell,* state government is responsible for education, health, transport, natural resources, the environment, law and order, and emergency services. *Finally,* the Federal Government is responsible for things that affect the whole of Australia, including defence, mining, trade, airports, post and telecommunications, social services, Medicare and currency. **From the information, we found out that** government in Australia is complicated.

NB information not included

questions to help you summarise

- Do I know the difference between a main point and a detail?
- Have I separated the mains ideas from the details?
- Do I know which information is important?
- Why have I not included certain information?
- Why is summarising information an important skill?

planning for summarising

hand organiser for key points

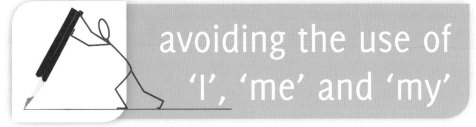

avoiding the use of 'I', 'me' and 'my'

explanation:

Sometimes, it is fine to use 'I', 'me' or 'my', especially if you are writing about yourself or something that you did. However, in some subjects such as Science, History, Geography and Technology your writing reads better if you do not use 'I', 'me' or 'my'. Here are some words and phrases to help you develop this skill.

ways of saying

It seems as though ...

It can be seen ...

It is clear that ...

The facts show that ...

This reveals that ...

This shows that ...

Therefore, it can be claimed that ...

This is obvious because ...

The author states that ...

It is obvious that ....

Evidence suggests that ...

It means that ...

It appears as though ...

avoiding the use of said

admitted	gasped	observed	shouted
agreed	giggled	offered	shrieked
announced	gulped	pleaded	sighed
answered	grunted	promised	smirked
argued	hissed	proposed	snapped
asked	mentioned	protested	sneered
babbled	inquired	queried	sobbed
began	insisted	questioned	spoke
blurted	interjected	quipped	sputtered
bragged	interrupted	quoted	stammered
called	jeered	ranted	stated
claimed	joked	reasoned	suggested
commented	laughed	reassured	taunted
complained	lied	remembered	teased
congratulated	mimicked	reminded	told
cried	moaned	repeated	urged
declared	mumbled	replied	uttered
denied	murmured	requested	vowed
dictated	muttered	retorted	whimpered
drawled	nagged	roared	whispered
exclaimed	noted	scolded	wondered
explained	objected	screamed	yelled

avoiding the use of 'and then'

after	finally	next
also	first, second, third	now that
as	following/followed by	once
as a final point	formerly	on top of
as well as	initially	previously
as soon as	in summary	prior to
at the outset	in the beginning	subsequently
at the same time	later on	the next day/week/year
before	meanwhile	ultimately
every time	moreover	up until now

key task word glossary

account for	to give reasons for something and report on those reasons
analyse	to look at the parts of something and show how the parts connect to each other
argue or persuade	to give an opinion on a topic and try to persuade others of your point of view by giving evidence and using persuasive techniques
arrange	to place things into a particular position or order
assess	to make a judgment about something based on its value or worth
break down	to take something large and examine the parts of it and how they link to one another
compare	to look at two or more things and say how they are similar and different
conclude	to draw together the main points and state them in a brief way
connect	to link ideas or people because they have things in common
consider	to give opinions about the information you have been given about someone or something
contrast	to look at two or more things and say how they are different
criticise	to make judgments about someone or something, giving details to support your views
debate	to look at both sides of an issue and decide the 'right' side or persuade a listener/reader to accept the better argument
decide	to choose something or someone after considering other options

key task word glossary

describe	to tell the reader about someone or something; include the features or characteristics
discuss	to look at both sides of an issue—does not always reach a conclusion
distinguish	to make note of the differences between things
draw together	to bring ideas together to come to a conclusion
evaluate	to weigh up the value or worth of something
examine	to look at something or someone very carefully—often to find out 'how' or 'why' something may have happened
explain (how)	to make the reader understand the process of how something works or occurs, usually in a series of steps
explain (why)	to make the reader understand why something is the way it is by giving reasons
generalise	to develop a broad statement that can apply to many things
give more detail	to look at something in a more detailed way by giving more information
identify	to notice something or someone and the features of it
illustrate	to use examples of something to give more detail to information or more weight to an argument
infer	to work something out even though it is not said or written
interpret	to explain the meaning or significance of something
justify	to give reasons for a decision or conclusion that has been made; answering the question, 'Why?'
link	to make a connection between things or people
list	to arrange items in order, usually one after the other
locate information	to find the information that is stated; the information is 'right there'

key task word glossary

(to) make connections	to make meaning by connecting ideas with own experiences and across paragraphs and illustrations in text
make a decision	to examine a number of options and come to a conclusion about the best one
outline	to give all the main ideas about something without the details
propose	to put forward an idea or plan for others to think about
provide support	to give evidence or examples to support an idea, fact or opinion
put it together	to connect ideas across text or draw ideas from several places or sources
reflect	to look back and think about what something means to you or the effect that it has on you as a learner
retell/recount	to arrange events in the order in which they happened; sequence is important
review	to go over something or look at something for the second time
sequence	giving a series of steps in the order in which they occur
solve (problems)	to develop solutions to problems based on their causes and effects
sort	to place things or people in groups because of what they have in common
state	to name something or make it clear to the listener/reader
suggest	to put forward an idea or plan – usually so that other people can think about it
summarise	to briefly state the main message/idea/subject without details
support	to back up an idea or point of view by giving evidence and examples

modality table

	least intense ➤ most intense			
how certain	might	maybe	could	will
how often	never	sometimes	often	always
how likely	unlikely	possible/ly	probable/ly	definitely
how important	unimportant	required	necessary	essential
how sure	unsure	apparently	clearly	postive/ly

my useful words and phrases

my useful words and phrases

my useful words and phrases

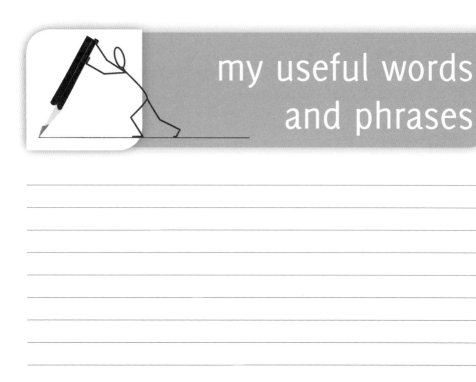

my useful words and phrases

cluster map

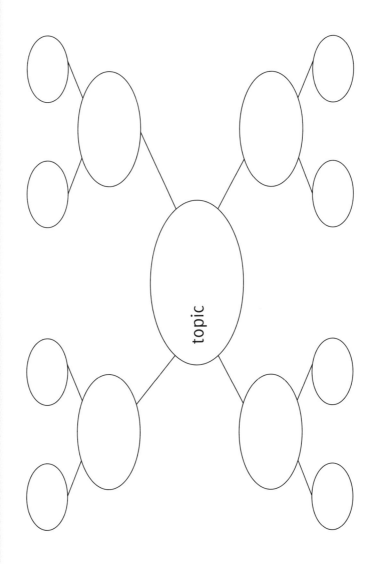

topic

reasons for and against

topic

reason for

reason for

reason for

contrast connectives: on the other hand, whereas, however, by contrast, even though, etc.

reason against

reason against

reason against

64

classification table

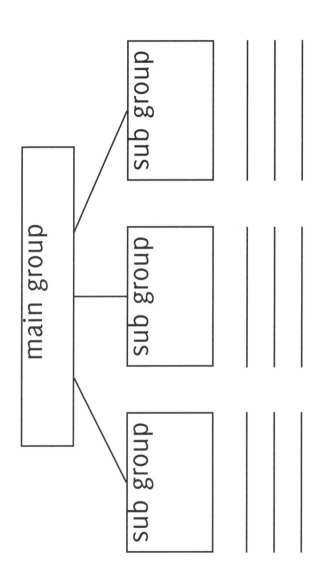

3 column Venn

I am comparing .... with ....

how different?	how the same?	how different?

contrast matrix

	object 1	object 2
characteristic 1		
characteristic 2		
characteristic 3		

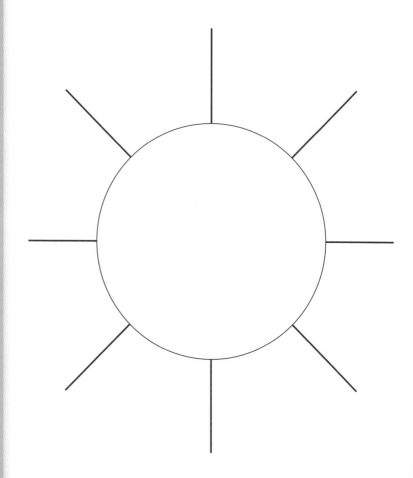

spider chart

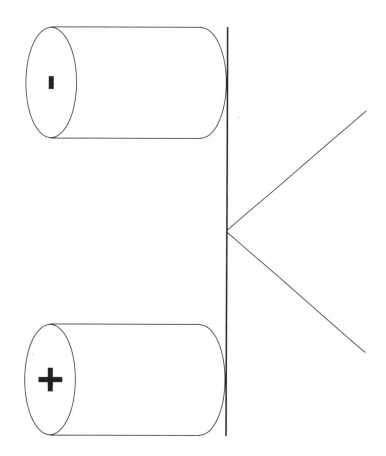

cause effect table

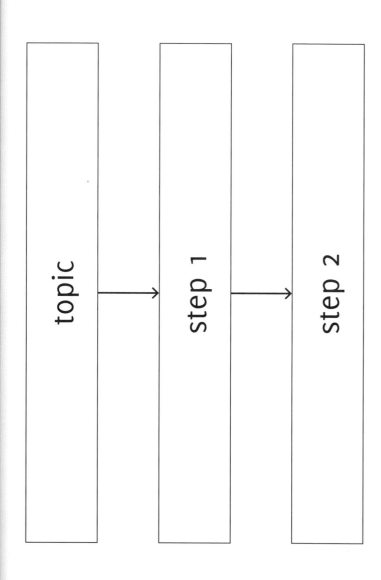

topic	step 1	step 2

cause effect table

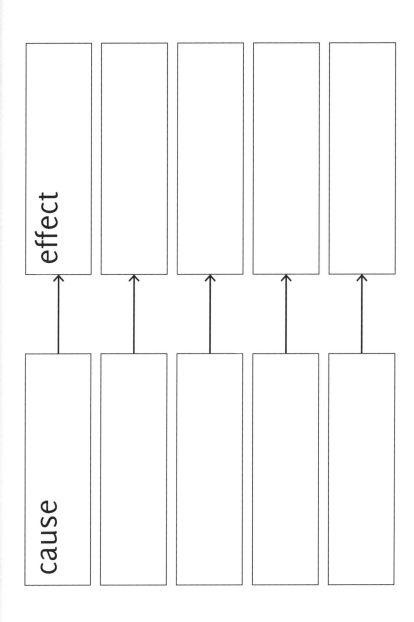

cause

effect

generalising funnel

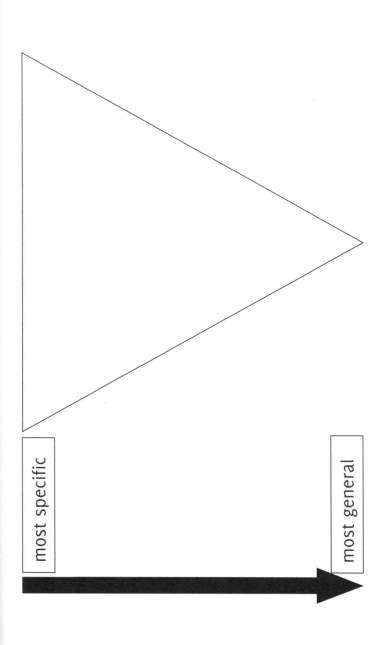

most specific

most general

iceberg for giving more detail

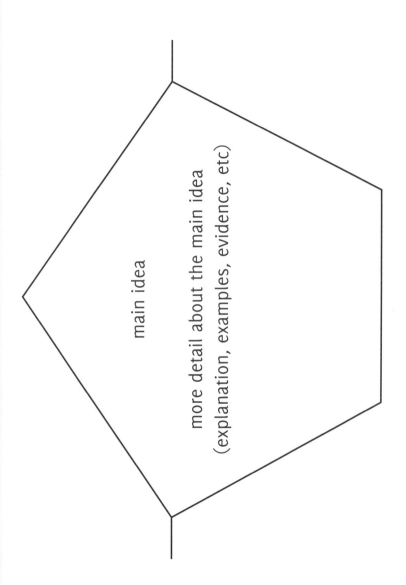

main idea

more detail about the main idea
(explanation, examples, evidence, etc)

inference organiser

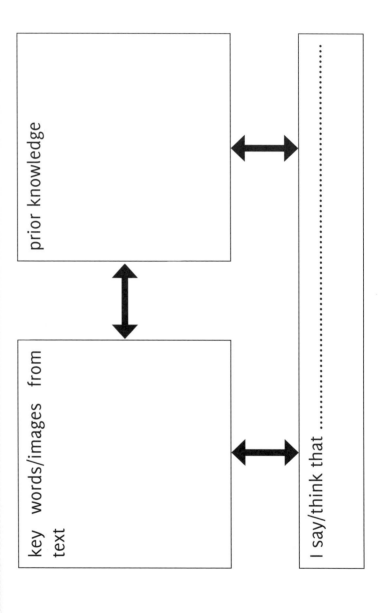

key words/images from text

prior knowledge

I say/think that ....

interpreting table

what I'm told	what it means	what I'm told	what it means

justification flow chart

decision:

justification:

because

because

because

list

list

1.

2.

3.

4.

5.

6.

7.

8.

9.

10.

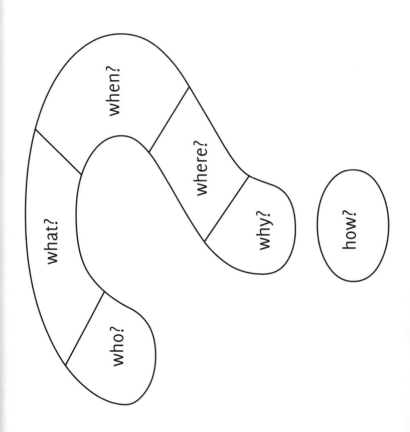

what?

when?

who?

where?

why?

how?

bringing it together template

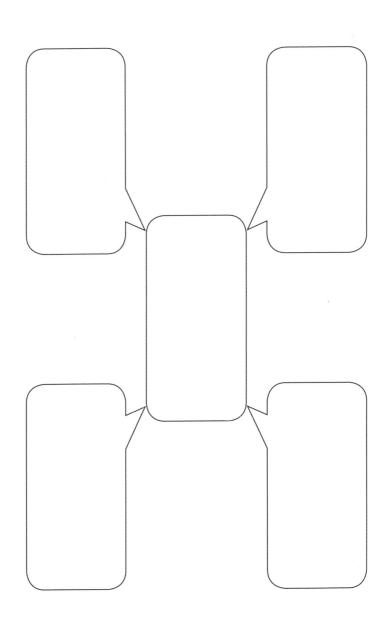

decision making matrix

alternative 1		alternative 2	
plus	minus	plus	minus
final decision			

supporting columns

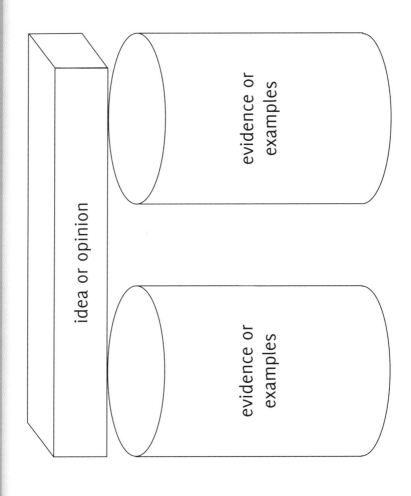

idea or opinion

evidence or examples

evidence or examples

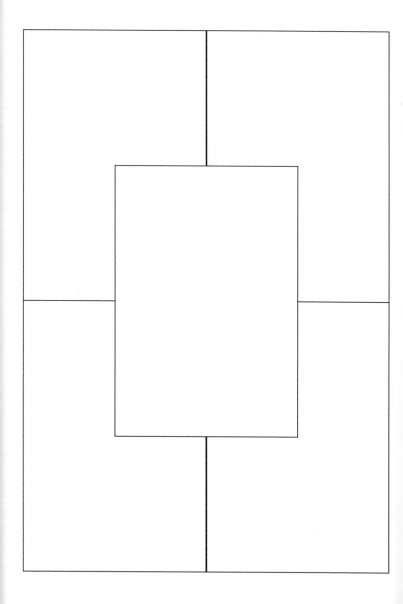

Frayer Model

PMI chart

	plus	minus	interesting
event/feature			
event/feature			
event/feature			

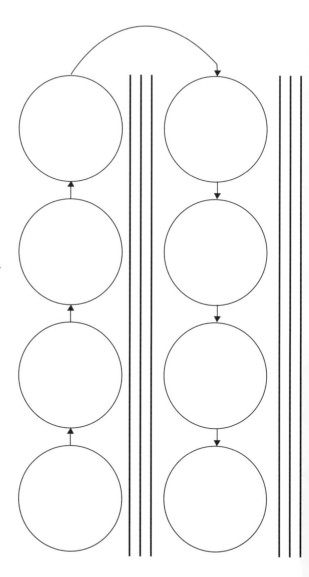

8 events

Direction: Draw pictures to represent 8 main events. Make sure they are in the order in which they happened (chronological order).

flow chart

direction: chart the steps/events that lead to others

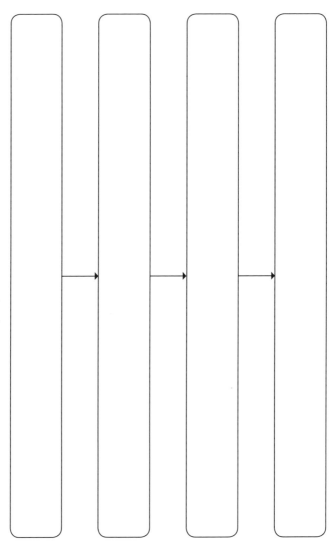

problem solution template 1

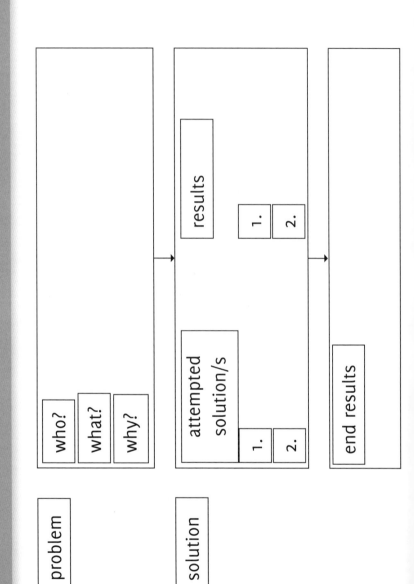

problem

| who? |
| what? |
| why? |

solution

attempted solution/s

1.

2.

results

1.

2.

end results

about the author

Catherine Black is an independent literacy consultant living in northern New South Wales. She specialises in literacy in-service and resources for upper primary and lower secondary teachers of all subject areas.

Catherine is a secondary teacher who has taught in Queensland, New South Wales and the United Kingdom.

Catherine believes that literacy is integral to all subject areas. Her aim is to help high school teachers, who traditionally have little training in literacy, to develop strategies to assist their students to come to terms with the literacy demands of their subjects.

For more information, contact Catherine on:

Mobile: 0428824626

Email: cablack75@gmail.com

about the author

Patricia Hipwell is an independent literacy consultant for her own company, **logonliteracy**. She delivers literacy professional development to teachers in Australia, and works predominantly in Queensland schools. Patricia has specialised in assisting all teachers to be literacy teachers, especially high school subject specialists who often struggle with what it means to be a content area teacher and a literacy teacher. Assessment has been an area of interest for many years and much of Patricia's work enables teachers to create assessment that is 'do-able'. Students often have very little idea of what they are required to do and rely heavily on parents/caregivers to assist them.

The idea for this book came from the success of, '**How to Write What You Want to Say**'; a middle years resource written to assist students who struggle with putting into words what they want to say, especially when the 'saying' involves writing. It has been Patricia's experience that students need help to develop the language that mature writers use. If we assist students with this in the primary years, they will be writers who are more confident when they enter high school. In this book, there are sentence starters and key connectives that students should use when demonstrating a particular writing skill. Language is the way that it is because of the job that it does, and letting students into the secret of this makes a significant difference to the quality of the work they produce.

Patricia has developed a number of resources to assist students' literacy development. She is available to provide professional development to teachers to support the use of the resources, including this one that she recommends.

For further information, contact:

Patricia Hipwell

Mobile 0429727313 | email: pat.hipwell@gmail.com

www.logonliteracy.com.au

Brisbane, Queensland 4075, Australia

2014

This book has been self-published by logonliteracy.

Also by Patricia Hipwell:

How to Write What You Want to Say

How to Write What You Want to Say ...
in mathematics
(co-authored with Lyn Carter)

Australian Shows and The Flying Doctors
(Oxford Literacy Guided Readers—
co-authored with Lyn Carter)